Arch 468 and Ovalhouse]

Cuddles

by Joseph Wilde

First produced in this version at Ovalhouse on Tuesday 14 May 2013

An earlier draft of the script was developed by Ironclad Theatre as part of the Capital Plays Festival

This playtext went to print before the end of the rehearsal process so may differ slightly from the version performed.

Published by Playdead Press 2013

© Joseph Wilde

Joseph Wilde has asserted his rights under the
Copyright, Design and Patents Act, 1988, to be
identified as the author of this work.

A CIP catalogue record for this book is available from
the British Library.

ISBN 978-0-9576077-5-0

Playdead Press
www.playdeadpress.com

Cuddles

by Joseph Wilde

Cast

EVE	Carla Langley
TABBY	Rendah Heywood

Creative Team

Writer	Joseph Wilde
Director	Rebecca Atkinson-Lord
Designer	James Turner
Lighting Designer	Pablo Baz
Sound Designer	Edward Lewis
Stage Manager on Book	Emily Russell
Assistant Director	Celeste Dring
Producer	Lucy Jackson
Publicity photographs	Alex Beckett
Production photographs	Paul Fox

This production has been supported by

Cast

CARLA LANGLEY // EVE

Carla graduated from Italia Conti on the BA (Hons) Acting course in July 2012.

She made her professional debut as Orlaith in the world-premiere of Desolate Heaven (Theatre503).

Other theatre includes As You Like It (Sam Wanamaker Festival, Shakespeare's Globe) and The Three Lives of Lucie Cabrol (Edinburgh Fringe Festival).

After Cuddles she joins the company of Liolà at The National Theatre, directed by Richard Eyre.

RENDAH HEYWOOD // TABBY

Theatre includes Hettie in The Kitchen directed by Bijan Sheibani, Belle/Ensemble in Rocket to the Moon directed by Angus Jackson, Tsvetaeva in Philistines directed by Howard Davies, Girl in The Rose Tattoo directed by Steven Pimlott/Nicholas Hytner and Ensemble in Therese Raquin directed by Marianne Elliott (all National Theatre), Maid in Ring Round the Moon (West End) directed by Sean Mathias for ACT Productions, Above and Beyond (Corinthia) and You Once Said Yes (Roundhouse) for Look Left Look Right, 22nd July Project (Ovalhouse) and Attempts on Her Life (BAC).

TV and Film includes The Bill, Holby City, EastEnders, Kill Keith and The Journey Home.

Creative Team

JOSEPH WILDE // PLAYWRIGHT

Cuddles is Joseph's first full-length play.

Last year his first radio play The Loving Ballad of Captain Bateman aired on BBC Radio 4.

Short plays include White Day (Allthepigs/New Diorama), The Hard Part (Chichester Festival Theatre), The Big Ask (finalist at OffCut Festival) and Zulu Wedding (winner of ScriptSpace at the Tobacco Factory).

He trained on the Young Writers Programmes of the Royal Court and Chichester Festival Theatre and is currently on a year-long attachment at HighTide Festival Theatre.

REBECCA ATKINSON-LORD // DIRECTOR

Rebecca trained as a Director at RADA and with Frantic Assembly, Complicite, Told by an Idiot, the Royal Opera House and at The Young Vic. Her work has taken her from major international companies like Shakespeare's Globe, Scottish Opera and the Royal Opera House, Covent Garden, to intimate found spaces in London and beyond.

As a writer-director, credits include Seeking Oblivion (BAC), Mrs Edna Way (Arch 468) and an original adaptation of Medea (Barons Court Theatre).

Directing includes The Sluts of Sutton Drive (Finborough Theatre), Mother Clap's Molly House and

The Flies (Crescent Theatre, Birmingham), Romeo and Juliet (Teatro Technis), Five Eleven (King's Head Theatre and Tour) and numerous new plays by emerging writers including Janice Okoh, Chad Armistead and Louise Monaghan at venues including Arch 468 and Theatre503. She is Director of Theatre at Ovalhouse and Founding Artistic Director and Chief Executive of Arch 468.

JAMES TURNER // DESIGNER
James trained on the Motley Theatre Design Course and works as an assistant to Ultz and Bunny Christie.
Designs include: Cause Celèbre (Central School of Speech and Drama), The Long Life and Great Good Fortune of John Clare (Eastern Angles, Tour), Beyond Beauty (The Last Refuge), A Life and The Sluts of Sutton Drive (Finborough Theatre), I Am a Camera and Execution of Justice (Southwark Playhouse), Strong Arm and That Moment (Underbelly, Edinburgh), The Ripple Effect (Richmond Theatre), Mercury Fur (Trafalgar Studios and Old Red Lion), The Fire Raisers, Oh What a Lovely War and Much Ado About Nothing (British American Drama Academy), Thrill Me (Tristan Bates Theatre and Charing Cross Theatre), Plain Jane (Royal Exchange Studio, Manchester), Some Stories (Templeworks, Leeds), Over the Moon (New Wimbledon Studio), No Wonder (Library Theatre, Manchester) and A Man of No Importance (Union Theatre and Arts Theatre). Upcoming work includes: The Golden Voice (Arts

Theatre). James won the 2013 Off-West-End Award for Best Set Designer for Mercury Fur.
www.jamesturnerdesign.com

PABLO BAZ // LIGHTING DESIGNER
Pablo Fernandez Baz trained at the Central School of Speech and Drama.

He is resident lighting designer for Zecora-Ura, winners of a Herald Angel Award for Hotel Medea (Edinburgh Festival Fringe) and Fourth Monkey, Off-West-End nomination 2012 for best lighting design for 4:48 Psychosis.

Pablo has recently worked with Simone Riccio (Mime Fest 2013), Talawa Theatre, Joseph Mercier, Karla Shacklock and Stonecrabs, and assisted Lighting Designer Adam Silverman at the ENO.

EDWARD LEWIS // SOUND DESIGNER AND COMPOSER
Edward studied Music at Oxford University and subsequently trained as a composer and sound designer at the Bournemouth Media School.

Theatre includes Gravity (Birmingham Rep Theatre), A Midsummer Night's Dream (Almeida), Molly Sweeney and Thom Pain (Print Room), On The Rocks, Amongst Friends, Ignorance and Darker Shores (Hampstead Theatre), Slowly, Hurts Given and Received and Apple Pie (Riverside Studios), Measure For Measure (Cardiff Sherman), Emo (Bristol Old Vic and Young Vic), Once

Upon A Time in Wigan and 65 Miles (Paines Plough/Hull Truck Theatre), Krapp's Last Tape and Spoonface Steinberg (Hull Truck), The Shallow End (Southwark Playhouse), I Am Falling (Sadler's Wells and The Gate, Notting Hill), Orpheus and Eurydice and Quartet (Old Vic Tunnels), The Beloved (The Bush), The Stronger, The Pariah, Boy With A Suitcase, Walking The Tightrope, Le Marriage and Meetings (The Arcola), Hedda and Breathing Irregular (The Gate, Notting Hill), Madness In Valencia (Trafalgar Studios), The Madness Of George III, Kalagora and Macbeth (National Tours), Othello (Rose Theatre, Bankside), Knives In Hens (Battersea Arts Centre), Personal Enemy (White Bear & New York), Accolade, Rigor Mortis, Fog, Don Juan Comes Back From The War, Perchance To Dream, Drama At Inish, In The Blood, The December Man, Beating Heart Cadaver, Blue Surge, The American Clock, His Greatness, Portraits, Laburnum Grove and Mirror Teeth (Finborough Theatre), as well as on the Arden Project for the Old Vic and the Vibrant season at the Finborough Theatre.

Edward has been nominated for several Off West End Theatre Awards, and films he has recently worked on have won several awards at the LA International Film Festival and Filmstock International Film Festival.

EMILY RUSSELL // STAGE MANAGER ON BOOK
Trained at Royal Holloway, University of London in Drama and Theatre Studies.

Stage Management includes The Drawer Boy, Cornelius and Everyday Maps for Everyday Use and I Didn't Always Live Here (Finborough Theatre), HAVERFORDWEST (TheSpace@Surgeons Hall), Something Good (Firestation Arts Centre) and various Drama Society productions at Royal Holloway.
Deputy Stage Management includes The Sluts of Sutton Drive (Finborough Theatre).

CELESTE DRING //ASSISTANT DIRECTOR

Celeste writes and performs as part of comedy group Lebensmüde, currently artists in residence at The Last Refuge, Peckham, where they produce regular comedy nights.

Directing includes A Flawed Connection (Drayton Arms scratch), Everybody Dance Now (Central Youth Theatre), Webb (BAC scratch) and Joy (Brockley Jack scratch).

Assistant directing includes The Sluts of Sutton Drive (Finborough Theatre) and Britain's Got Bhangra (Watford Palace Theatre).

Celeste also worked on The Royal Court's Theatre Local project.

LUCY JACKSON // PRODUCER

Lucy Jackson is a freelance producer and project manager. Theatre includes Mudlarks (HighTide Festival, Theatre503 & Bush Theatre), Fanta Orange and Don Juan Comes Back From the War at the Finborough

Theatre, as well as the theatre's Vibrant – A Festival of Finborough Playwrights festivals (2009, 2010 and 2011). For Offstage Theatre Lucy produced Amphibians (Bridewell Theatre), for Misshapen Theatre she produced Phillipa and Will are Now in a Relationship and The Sexual Awakening of Peter Mayo (Pleasance Edinburgh and Theatre 503) and Blast Off (Theatre503 & Soho Theatre), and for Rogues' Gallery she produces The Folk Contraption (VAULT Festival/London Wonderground/Latitude Festival). She was a producer at Old Vic New Voices for The 24 Hour Plays, The TS Eliot US/UK Exchange (The Old Vic) and Time Warner Ignite 4 (Waterloo East). She has produced and managed at seven Edinburgh Festival Fringes including And No More Shall We Part for Hampstead Theatre (Traverse Theatre), PEEP for Natural Shocks, White Rabbit, Red Rabbit (Volcano Theatre) and Thom Tuck Goes Straight-to-DVD (Fosters Edinburgh Comedy Award Nominee for Best Newcomer). She is Producing Associate for New York-based company the TEAM, and has been a Production Assistant for TEG Productions /Jeremy Meadow Ltd. Lucy is currently a Stage One Apprentice for Mark Rubinstein Ltd.

Arch468

"Arch 468 is a laboratory for incubating the theatre of the future"
Evening Standard

Arch 468 explores new ways to make and think about theatre. We help emerging artists of all ages to explore and refine their own best practice by giving them the resources and freedom to flop or fly.

Arch 468 aims to celebrate new theatre and the headstrong courage of young artists and provide a hub where emerging artists can meet to develop their work, challenge themselves and find bold new audiences.

Since opening in 2008, Arch 468 has provided more than £80,000 worth of free development time, space and resources to emerging theatre makers and continues to be a key venue supporting the burgeoning new-theatre scene.

As producer Arch 468 makes theatre that blazes new trails to shape the arts ecology of the future.

Arch468.com | @BexArch468

LOTTERY FUNDED

Supported using public funding by
ARTS COUNCIL ENGLAND

OVALHOUSE

Anti-heroes and underdogs.
Stories told sideways.
The things under the bed.
Theatre for people with something to say.
New work for new audiences.

Since the 1960s, Ovalhouse has been a pioneering supporter of queer, feminist and diverse performance work. We remain committed to challenging preconceptions of what theatre is and can be.

Ovalhouse's current programme embodies our commitment to true artistic diversity, our appetite for experimentation with form and our dedication to process.

ovalhouse.com | @ovalhouse

Supported using public funding by
**ARTS COUNCIL
ENGLAND**

Lambeth

GODS & MONSTERS
Ovalhouse Summer 2013

Bears, vampires, explorers.

Journeys in search of illusive certainty.

Belief systems that sit on the border between imagination and reality.

Gods + Monsters is a season of adventures in live performance that asks which is which; and why, even in an age of twenty-four hour news and online shopping, both gods and monsters seem so essential to the way we define ourselves.

Cuddles by Joseph Wilde | 14 May – 1 June 2013

The Bear by Angela Clerkin & Improbable | 21 May – 8 June 2013

The Ted Bundy Project by Greg Wohead | 24 & 25 May 2013

Taranis by Paper Tiger | 1 June 2013

Adventure/Misadventure by Nick Field | 4-22 June 2013

Shield by Amaara Raheem | 11-29 June 2013

[1]

A small room. No windows. A child-sized bed. Two bins: one red, one green. The floor is covered with layers of newspaper.
Years without natural light has stained everything with gloom; except for a pile of almost new looking books.
EVE, a pale, emaciated, faintly androgynous teenager, sits on her own – a canary in a mineshaft.

EVE   Once Upon a Time a wealthy old king lived in a faraway land, with his beautiful queen and his cherished daughter. The Princess.
Though the King and Queen doted on her in all things, they longed for a son. Because only sons can inherit a kingdom.

Each night the storks flew over the house in a great cloud
But never once did they leave a child behind.

Thirteen summers turned to thirteen winters and still the sheets were barren.
The Queen grieved and the King cursed.
He cursed the earth and the sky, he cursed the waters and the winds. He cursed the forests and the oceans and every living thing.
He cursed himself.

2

And silently, in her chamber lacquered in
gold and silver and more jewels than there
are ants in the grass
The cherished Princess secretly wished for
a baby sister
To share her secrets.

Then one howling and stormful night
When fire tore the sky to ribbons
And the storks feared to take to wing
A baby was found in the old king's bed.

A baby girl.

The King's heart ached and the Queen
quailed.
For, they wondered, if the storks did not
bring them this baby
Then what creature had?

As the cuckoo child grew and gaped and
hungered and keened
They wailed and they wept. They hid her
away where she could bring no harm, as
was right
And prayed to God to save them, as was
also right.
But up in the room above the attic in the
only tower taller than the tallest tower,
the monster grew.

The Queen fled the kingdom
To shack up with another king with more
money and better teeth.
Who owned a Bentley and luxury villa.

In Tuscany.

Wracked with guilt and wrenched with
grief the old king became bitter and
haunted.
He cursed the cuckoo, he cursed the
princess and he cursed all women.
He cursed holes in the castle and cursed
great cuts in the earth.

He cursed black and cursed blue, until the
curses strangled his heart.
So the Princess inherited the kingdom
after all. And she inherited the cuckoo
monster too.

But the princess knew better than her
parents. She knew the monster was not
really a monster at all, but her little wish-
sister.
She loved her and kept her secret and kept
her safe
And raised her all alone.

TABBY   And?

TABBY, early 30s, dressed for work, her hair in a business-like bun, emerges from the shadows.
She squats next to EVE and strokes her.

EVE   And
             And they lived happily after.

TABBY kisses her.

TABBY   More or less.

TABBY checks her watch and exits.

EVE   Tabby takes care of me.
             Protects me. Cleans me.
             Feeds me.
             Every day she rides out of the castle to do
             battle with the darkness and keep us safe.
             Except at weekends.

TABBY enters and sits. She is in her office at work. She speaks into an intercom.

TABBY   You can send Mr Wallace in now.

EVE   She would do anything for me.

TABBY   Hi Graham. Welcome to my shiny new
             office.
             What do you think?

You've been a loyal servant of this company for so many years, you must have seen a few changes.

I bet, for example, that you never expected to see me here.

In this office. In this

Very.

Nice.

Chair.

No. In fact I think you've had *your* beady eye on this office for some time.

But there we are. That's the way the cookie arse-fucks you. Right?

Please. Have a seat.

I'm joking. Stand the fuck up. God.

Now. Graham. Before we go any further allow me to make one thing clear

I appreciate the way you looked out for me after Daddy died.

Taught me the tricks of the trade as it were. You really took me under your wing. Well. Your desk.

You did me quite a few favours. You taught me everything I needed to know: do this, do that, suck this, touch that.

Yes I think I can still taste your 'favours'.

But look at me now.
And look at you.

OK enough of that Graham, we can do this the hard way.
Or we can do this the abject
Excruciating
Horrifying way.

Oh come on you must have seen this coming. You must appreciate your position here has now become
Untenable.

Don't
Oh don't cry Graham for God's sake.

I'm fucking you this time.
Take it like a man.

EVE   Tabby's the best sister in the world.

She taught me to read.
My favourite book is *Harry Potter* even though I know bits of it probably aren't even real.

[2]

EVE   She's coming back

TABBY enters.

                What's the password?

TABBY stops.

TABBY   Oh for God's-
                9-7-5-3

EVE   Eve is safe Eve is free

TABBY   Thank fuck it's Friday.

EVE   Yay!
                Cuddles?

TABBY   Yes please. Level 5.

EVE   Level 5 Cuddles - initiate!

She leaps onto TABBY, embracing her.
She notices TABBYs exposed neck.

                Tabby scarf

TABBY   Ohshitshit

8

TABBY throws EVE off her. EVE lunges for TABBY's neck, but TABBY deflects her with the practised efficiency of a martial artist.

EVE   Downward Dog!

EVE throws herself into the yoga pose and TABBY rummages in her bag for her scarf, tying it round her neck.

TABBY   There. All better.

               Eve?

EVE doesn't move.

EVE   It's the Hunger.

TABBY   I know.

EVE   Need blood

TABBY   I know Eve don't bang on about it

EVE   You're late.

TABBY   I know

EVE   Fifty five thousand one hundred and eleven heartbeats.

TABBY   I know I got held / up

EVE   I was scared you wouldn't come back. And
               then I'd be alone and I'd starve and I'd
               have to eat my own feet and then my own
               legs and my own bad bits and my own
               body and arms and neck until when you
               came back I'd just be a head. Screaming.

TABBY   OK.
               But I did. I did come back.
               I always do.
               OK?
               I always will. Remember?

EVE   Where did you go?

TABBY   Eve. I

               I was attacked.

EVE   No!

TABBY   Yes! By a Chugger.

EVE   What's a Chugger?

TABBY   Sit down and I'll tell you.

               OK

Chuggers are creatures that once upon a time used to be people.
But nobody loved them. Nobody cared for them.

EVE   Not like me

TABBY   No. There was no one to pay any attention to these poor people. So they grew up horrible and twisted, and came to feed on misery and guilt.

EVE   What do they look like?

TABBY   Well they come in all shapes and sizes but you can always spot a Chugger by the brightly-coloured twatty little bibs they wear.

EVE   Where do they live?

TABBY   Wherever there is misery and guilt to feed on.
               Near stations mostly.

EVE   And they attacked you?

TABBY   One of them did. Yes.

EVE   How did you defeat it?

TABBY   To defeat a Chugger
          What you do is
          You tell them to leave you alone. In a firm
          loud voice.

          And if that doesn't work you grab them by
          their little twat-bib and you stamp your
          heel down onto their instep until you hear
          it crack.

          And
          And it's a shame because he was sort of
          pretty and now he'll probably press
          charges and now I have to go to the
          hospital and I hate fucking hospitals and I
          just want to throw myself down a well or a
          a a sewer somewhere wet and dark and
          endless

EVE   You don't sound very happy Tabby.

          I can see it.

TABBY   See what.

EVE   Sad Face.
          Turn that frown around.

          Shall I sing you a song?

12

TABBY   No.
               No thank you Evee.

EVE begins to massage her shoulders.

               That's
               That's nice.

EVE   Why are you sad?

TABBY   It's
               It's Mr Wallace.

EVE hisses.

EVE   The demon!

TABBY   Yes.

EVE   What happened?

TABBY   I
               I defeated him.

EVE   What?

TABBY   I beat him. It's over. He's gone.
               I ripped his black heart out and threw it
               on a fire.
               I

13

EVE	You defeated the Mr Wallace?
TABBY	Yes.
EVE	Wow!
	Wowee!
	But. That's good isn't it?
TABBY	Fourteen years too late.
EVE	How did you defeat the Mr Wallace?
TABBY	What's rule number 7?
EVE	But you
TABBY	What's rule number 7?
EVE	Don't ask questions about the Mr Wallace.
TABBY	Right then.
EVE	But why aren't you happy?
TABBY	Why aren't I happy? Why aren't I?
EVE	Tabby?

TABBY   Well it doesn't matter does it? It's done
               now so
               Fuck that. Move on.

EVE   I made you something.

TABBY   Oh?

EVE   I made it out of my hair. Shall I show
               you?

TABBY   Not now sweetie.

EVE   Are you sure you don't want me to sing /
               to you

TABBY   Please Eve. I just want to

TABBY looks into the green bin.

TABBY   To

               Eve

               EVE

EVE   Yes?

TABBY   What is this?

15

EVE   Green bin.

TABBY   What's the green bin for?

EVE   Wee wee.

TABBY   Piss, Eve, you sound like a fucking retard.
                 It's for piss.

                 So why
                 Is there
                 A fucking
                 Turd in it.

                 Rule number 8 the / red

EVE   The red bin is for poo.

TABBY   Look Eve.
                 LOOK
                 What can you see?

EVE   Angry face.

TABBY   That's right.
                 You know the rules. You know the fucking
                 rules
                 Do I need to get The Leash? I think I do.

EVE   No Tabby

She grabs EVE and pinches her. EVE screams.

TABBY   Why Eve Why. It's basic it's fucking basic.
             Red and Green. Is that too much to ask?
             What do you think happens, what do you
             think happens if you break the fucking
             rules

TABBY lets go.
EVE rubs her arm.

             I do this
             I do this for you.

EVE   I'm sorry Tabby.
             I'm really sorry.

TABBY   Oh fuck. No. I'm sorry Evee. It's not your
             fault.
             I'm just
             I have had a really shitty day

EVE   It's ok.

TABBY   Is it?

EVE   I know.
             I'll Close My Eyes.

TABBY   Not now Evee.

17

EVE stands with her eyes closed.

TABBY sighs.

          OK. Close Your Eyes.

EVE   Already have.

TABBY   Shh. The magic's working.
          Where's the hole?

EVE places her hand over her solar plexus.

TABBY   Let me find you a soul.

          Here. Here it is. Nice and fresh.
          It's warm. It's tiny and completely perfect.

EVE   Like me.

TABBY   Like you.
          Shall I put it in?

EVE   Wait.

          Yes.

TABBY   In it goes.

EVE   It feels tingly.

TABBY	Can you feel it filling your body?
EVE	Eating up all the darkness.
TABBY	Does it hurt?
EVE	No it sads.
TABBY	Sads? Saddens?
EVE	It saddens. I can feel love.
TABBY	Here comes the mirror. Can you see?
EVE	I'm beautiful.
TABBY	Yes you are.
EVE	I'm a princess.
TABBY	I can see.
EVE	I'm Princess Eilonwy wife of High King Taran
TABBY	Ah

EVE   I'm a sorceress

TABBY   OK

EVE   But I'm also skilled with bow and sword
           and spear

TABBY   OK.
           Alright Eve

EVE   Eilonwy.

TABBY   OK Eilonwy shall we

EVE   Go outside.

TABBY   Can you see the door?

EVE   I'm walking through it

TABBY   Slow down Eve.
           It's creaking open.

EVE   Sunlight!

TABBY   Does it burn?

EVE   No it feels warm.

TABBY   Shall I hold your hand?

EVE   I'm not scared.
               There are trees everywhere.

TABBY   There are no trees in Loughton. They've
               been banished to the wild places.

EVE   I'm not in Loughton.

               I come here all the time.
               There's people here and no one is afraid,
               none of them want to kill me.

TABBY   Am I there too?

EVE   Of course you're here, you're talking to
               me.

TABBY   Of course.

EVE   I wish I could stay forever but the magic is
               running out.

TABBY   Come back inside quick, let me catch the
               soul. We don't want to lose it.

EVE opens her eyes.

EVE   Did you get it?

TABBY   Yes.

EVE   Can I see it?

TABBY   You know you can't.

EVE   Smell it?

TABBY   Souls don't smell.

EVE   Why?

TABBY   Because. Kiss it goodbye.

EVE does so. TABBY releases it.

               We'll see it again.

EVE   We'll see it again.

Silence.

               Can we have dinner?

TABBY   Yeah OK.

EVE   Dinner dinner?

TABBY   Oh. Not tonight sweetie, not tonight
               please

EVE   Why?

22

TABBY	I've had a long day sweetie and I have to go out again tomorrow.
EVE	Why?
TABBY	To go to the hospital.
EVE	Why?
TABBY	To find the Chugger and make sure he never bothers us again.
EVE	Oh. Good. What's a hospital?
TABBY	It's a place people go to get better.
EVE	Can people get better?
TABBY	Eve if you ask too many questions the Why Bird will peck out your eyeballs.
EVE	Yes I know. Will you read me a story?
TABBY	OK. After sandwiches. And just one.
EVE	Three

TABBY	One
EVE	Two
TABBY	One
EVE	One and a half
TABBY	EVE
EVE	Rapunzel?
TABBY	The one with the hair? No. Not after last time.
EVE	Cinderella?
TABBY	No Ugly Sisters please.
EVE	Ugly Ugly Duckling?
TABBY	Are there any Princesses in it?
EVE	Nope.
TABBY	Any Princes with adjectives instead of names?
EVE	Nope.

TABBY   Dwarves? Pixies? Does anyone get
              married?

EVE   No people in it at all.

TABBY   Well.
              That's a fucking start.

[3]

EVE is alone. TABBY in the hospital. She holds flowers, looking down at someone in a bed.

EVE   These are the rules.
            If a break them may my eyes rot in my
            skull
            May my teeth be torn out by the root
            May maggots nest in my lungs
            May my spine be injected with sulphuric
            acid
            And may my bad bits be devoured by
            diseased rats.

TABBY   Don't worry. I've not come to finish you
            off.
            How is the foot?

EVE   Rule number 13: Never bite the neck.
            Rule number 12: Don't cheat at monopoly
            Rule number 11: Don't scare Eve with
            crucifixes, garlic or holy water (I made
            that one up)

TABBY   Here. They were cheap.

EVE   Rule number 10: Say nice things or say
            nothing at all.

26

TABBY	My name's Tabitha. You look better. You know, without the twat-bib.
EVE	Rule number 9: Don't draw attention to yourself.
TABBY	Anyway. The flowers were cheap because out-of-court settlements are fucking expensive. That's the price you pay for living in a fair society. I say fair. Really I mean petty and litigious. But there we are.
EVE	Rule number 8: Don't say sorry unless you really really mean it.
TABBY	Mostly it's the price I pay for stamping on people. Ha ha Even if they are massively annoying tossers. Don't apologise you twat.
EVE	Rule number 7: Don't ask questions about the Mr Wallace
TABBY	So how much do you want?

EVE   Rule number 6: Green bin is for wee red
               bin is for poo

TABBY   Oh go on. Just take the money. You can
               use it to build a castle on your moral high
               ground.

EVE   Rule number 5: Don't hide things

TABBY   Don't make this difficult.
               I can afford big scary butt-fucking lawyers.
               If I have to. I will take you apart.
               I am thinking of you here.
               Drag me through the courts I will make a
               point of rinsing you so let's not.

EVE   Rule number 4: Don't lie

TABBY   Well would you like to posit a fucking
               counter-offer or am I wasting my time?

               Excuse me?

EVE   Rule number 3: Don't trust humans,
               except for Tabby and definitely not BOYS

TABBY   Is it the drugs, the morphine or

               You?
               A date?

One date?

And if IF I agree, you promise not to press charges?

EVE   Rule number 2: Don't let anyone in.

TABBY   Jesus I've met some desperate people but
            I mean you're not it's not like you're ugly
            or
            But if that's what you want. If that's how
            you want to play it.

EVE   Rule number 1:

TABBY   I'll see you in fucking court.

EVE   Never ever leave the safe place.

TABBY   Give me those.

TABBY takes the flowers and storms out.

EVE   But.
            Sometimes I see footprints. Little bare feet.
            One left one right.
            Shining. Like snail-trails.
            They walk across the floor up the wall and
            across the ceiling and down the wall and
            then. Out. Under the door.

29

And then I realise they are my footprints.
And I follow them.
Out of the safe place. Out through the
castle. Past the walls.
Out of Loughton. Into Albion.
Into the Wild Places.

I can walk for miles.
Into the mists and the marshes where the
giants' daughters walk.
The short cracked shouts of unseen hook-
beaked birds.
Where the plants and earth shiver with
business
Of millions of things living their short
amazing lives

The sunshine feels like warm water on my
skin.
I tread on soft green meadows. Clutch wet
earth with my toes.
Ride with the wild white horses and
scatter the birds before me.
Watch them warble and rise shrieking.
I stick to the path through the trees.
Though the wolf tempts me.
His thick hair bristles and hot damp
breaths. Claws scrape on my skin. Under
my clothes. He touches my bad bits and
we howl.

I pick the larkspur and forget-me-not; the monkshood and snow-on-the-mountain. And I put them in my hair.

I could walk the world.
South to scale Mount Olympus or north to the frozen mouth of Ginnungagap.
East to the Great Wall or West to Ground Zero and the Gap in the Sky.

Or I could just wander.
Through the tree lands. Tabby and me.
Where the people aren't afraid and no one wants to kill me.
And everyone who passes by
I just smile.

And they smile back.

And I can ask them questions and touch them
And then they
They touch me too.

[4]

EVE   Tabby's late again.
               No need to panic.

She tries to get her toe into her mouth. She can't.
TABBY is in the park. She has a bag of bread.

TABBY   OK. One. I'm here to complete my half of
               the deal. I am under no obligation to
               pretend to enjoy myself.
               Two. No photos, recordings or fucking
               Tweets.
               Three. If you try and sue me after this I
               will end your days. Understood?

EVE   Sometimes I think
               What if she doesn't come back this time?

TABBY   Right then. As long as you don't get the
               wrong idea.
               I'd hate you to think I was having fun.
               You've got one hour.

TABBY starts to throw bread to the ducks.
EVE begins to pick up the crumbs of bread and eat them.

EVE   Only three things kill vampires.
               Sunlight. Decapitation. Hammer a stake
               through the heart.

That works on nearly anything I bet.

TABBY
I like ducks. Straightforward little fuckers.
They gang-rape sometimes. Did you know
that?
Ducks.
They pair off naturally but come mating
season, any leftover males get into gangs
find an isolated female and chase her down
Fucking
Peck her. Into submission.
Take turns on her.

It's called 'rape flight'.

Just the males though.
Just the males.

EVE
We can't starve to death Tabby says but
the Hunger never stops.
So I'd get thinner and thinner, eating
myself. Getting weaker, my teeth falling
out
Skin stretched tight and dry over my
bones
And all the time the Hunger beating
against my ribs

But never dying.

33

TABBY	Time's running out Steve. How long are you going to let me twat on about ducks?
	I'd at least like to find somewhere with a loo first.
	Because I'm not doing it in the bushes like a fucking animal what sort of girl do you think I am.
EVE	Not going to let that happen.

She looks under the bed.

	Rule number 5. Don't hide things.
	But
	They're only little
TABBY	Come on Steve. You're cunt-struck. It's fine.
	I'm used to having men sniffing round my crotch. It's all the pretence I can't stand.
	You blackmailed me into sleeping with you. I get that. That's business.
	But I'm getting pretty bored watching you hobble around trying to hide your erection so just shit or get off the pot.
EVE	The first time it happened I thought I was dying. But Tabby knew what to do.
	Now I know it's a gift.

TABBY	Yes you did you said You did Steve. You did. You Well what the fuck do you want then?
EVE	Maybe I'm not a very good vampire.
TABBY	Bullshit
EVE	My teeth aren't even that sharp
TABBY	No. Bullshit.
EVE	And I feel Things.
TABBY	Why would I be upset? Why would I be upset Steve? Jesus. I did my bit so. Date over. Fuck off now and if you try and sue me I will have you killed.
EVE	I want
TABBY	I don't know what you think this is Steve but Do not. Do not contact me again.

EVE   I want

TABBY   Do you understand?
           Here be fucking monsters

EVE   I want to be

[5]

EVE   I want to be the iron.
            No! The top hat I want to be the top hat!

TABBY   You can be the top hat.

They are playing Monopoly.

EVE   What are you going to be?
            Tabby?
            Tabby what are you going to be?

TABBY   I am going to be
            The fucking
            Boot.

EVE   Me first.

            Yes!

            Your turn.

            Tabby.

            Your turn.

            Tabby.

            TABBY

TABBY   Alright Eve fucking hell.

She rolls. EVE begins grinding herself absently on the floor.

               What?
               Tax what the fuck
               When does that ever happen on the first
               turn?

EVE   You have to pay two hundred pounds.

TABBY   I know what tax means Eve you spiteful
               little bitch.

               What are you doing?
               Eve ew! What are you doing?

EVE   Just rubbin'

TABBY   Well stop it it's weird.

EVE   Feels good.

TABBY   Fine but. No. No stop it you're like a dog
               with worms. Yuk.
               Eve

               Do I need to get The Leash?

EVE stops.

Jesus.

Your turn.

EVE   Chance!
You win second prize in a beauty contest.
£15 from EVERY player

TABBY looks at her. Tension. She witheringly hands over £15.

EVE   Tabby?
Could I?

TABBY   What? What do you want?

EVE   Could I do you think?
Win second prize in a beauty contest.

TABBY   Oh. Well. I suppose it depends on the contest. You're not really the Miss World type. But you know. Some fashion models literally torture themselves to be as pale and interesting as you.

EVE   Hmmmm.

Your turn.

Tabby?

39

TABBY   What
               What about me?

EVE   Huh?

TABBY   How would I do in a beauty contest?
               Second prize?

               Third?
               Jesus fourth? Throw me a bone Eve.

EVE   First prize.

TABBY   Liar.

EVE   You're a princess.

TABBY   Look at me. Look
               Imagine you don't know me. What do you
               see?

EVE   You have nice eyes.

TABBY   Wrong. Try again.

EVE   Your smile is shiny.

TABBY   Is it? That's embarrassing.

EVE   And you smell nice. Your skin is soft and
             silky

TABBY   OK stop it it's getting weird now.

She rolls the dice.
She moves her piece.
EVE starts taking her turn.

             Could I be
             Jesus

EVE   What?

TABBY   Could I be loveable?
             I mean. If I wasn't so
             You know, all the time

EVE   I love you

TABBY   Yeah but
             Other people

EVE   Other people?

TABBY   I mean I'm your sister.

EVE   What other people?

41

TABBY   Forget it.
             My turn.

She takes her turn in silence.

EVE   Are you doing a think?

TABBY   Yes.

EVE   A good think or a bad think?

TABBY   I don't know.
             That's the thing about thinks.
             Your turn.

EVE takes her turn quietly.
TABBY mobile phone rings, in her handbag.

They listen to it for a while. EVE tries to locate the sound.
She is awed.

EVE   What's that?

TABBY   It's

             That

             That is a bird.

EVE   A bird?

TABBY   Yes a bird.

EVE   What's it called?

TABBY   It's a phoenix.

EVE   So that's what a phoenix sounds like.
             I've never heard one.

TABBY   They only come at very special times.

The ringing stops.

EVE   Wow...

TABBY   Eve

             Would you like to play a different game?
             I want to try something different.

[6]

TABBY is back in the park. EVE is doing yoga.

TABBY   Can you hear that? That's a blackbird.
Hear that?
Sounds nice though doesn't it?
That's its alarm call.
It's a warning. Listen.

EVE   Tabby taught me yoga. To control the
Hunger.

In through the nose.
Out through the mouth.

I thought about becoming vegan once
then I realised that was stupid.

TABBY   I don't look like it, but I could break your
arm.
If I wanted to. Trust me.
I'm built like a bull-dyke beneath the
fucking D and G.

EVE   Tabby is huge.
I don't mean fat. She's not fat.
But her love is huge.

TABBY   I could. But I choose not to.
               You could strangle me. Drag me into those
               bushes and rape me. But you choose not to.
               So thanks for that.

EVE   Sometimes I can't breathe. Her love fills
               the room. There's no space left for
               anything else. And
               And I want my love to be huge.

TABBY   Anything could happen.
               That dog could savage me. That car could
               Billions of little choices. Every day.

               That blackbird. Now
               If it suddenly decided to peck out my eyes.
               Would I be able to stop it?
               It would definitely have the element of
               surprise.

               And I would be standing here, half-blind
               for life
               Pissing blood from my eye-hole
               And crushing a blackbird to death with
               my big butch bull-dyke hands

               And a moment ago it was a perfectly
               ordinary day.

EVE   My love feels huge. In my chest but

               45

TABBY   But

EVE   But when I let it out

TABBY   But then there's you.

EVE   When I let it out it's just a bird
           A little hot white bird.
           And the further it gets from me the
           smaller it gets until I'm scared if it doesn't
           fly back inside me it will disappear

           Eaten up by the dark.

TABBY   I was ready for anything except you.

EVE   It's probably different for humans.
           If I was a princess...

TABBY   Now, who knows what will happen?
           You've broken the rules. You've opened
           the box.
           You're a crack in the wall.

EVE   Sleeping Beauty waited one hundred years
           for her Prince.
           Brunhilde slept in a ring of fire, on top of a
           mountain.
           Ishtar threw herself into the underworld
           itself.

TABBY It's none of your business really but I like
you.
Which is fucking stupid.
You should probably know that. I think.
For future reference.

EVE Vampires aren't supposed to love.
We don't give love we feed.

TABBY I just want you to know
I want you to know that I take no
responsibility for what happens now.

EVE If I had a Prince
Wouldn't have to worry about Tabby not
coming back.
Wouldn't need my gifts.

I could feed on him forever.

TABBY Whatever the fuck happens now.

[7]

TABBY sits. EVE is drinking blood from her arm.
TABBY strokes her hair.

TABBY   You have such soft hair. Why is that?
                   Mummy had great hair too the fucking
                   bitch. Why do you both get luscious glossy
                   Pantene Pro V locks and I get stuck with
                   Wiry dry muff-helmet.
                   It's not fair.

                   Nothing is.

EVE begins to grind herself gently against TABBY's leg.

                   This isn't how I expected life to pan out.
                   And you
                   You could have been a princess. A genius.
                   Loved by the world.
                   But the world's shit and you've got to piss
                   in a bin.

                   Except
                   You don't really do you. Not a bin.
                   You could

                   Uh.
                   Eve what are you

48

Are you humping my fucking leg?

Eve stop that!
EVE

TABBY tries to disengage herself from EVE but EVE bites down and won't be budged, grinding more furiously.

Ah! Fuck's sake Eve OW
Get off get off
Fucking
OFF

She jabs EVE in the eye. With a yelp EVE scuttles away from her.

EVE   My eye!

TABBY   Fucking / hell

EVE   You stabbed my eye

TABBY   You little bitch

TABBY clutches a bandage to her arm.

Fuck a duck.

EVE   Owww.

49

TABBY   Ok I just

She tries to stand but can't.

             OK whatever I'm just gonna
             Maybe I'll just

EVE   Tabby?

TABBY   I feel a bit

EVE   It's not my fault it's the Hunger

TABBY   Oh fuck off the Hunger you're just greedy
             Oh shit

EVE   Tabby? Tabby!

TABBY   Ah.
             Ah hah.

EVE   I'm sorry Tabby

TABBY   Think
             Think I'm going to have a little cry

EVE   Don't cry Tabby

TABBY   Just a little one

EVE	Tabby?
TABBY	Oh. Wow. Haven't cried in ten years. Not since I saw that tramp that looked just like Daddy. Stupid really. Should have just bought him a burger.
EVE	Tabby? What's wrong?
TABBY	Nothing. I need a little rest.
EVE	Cuddles?
TABBY	Um. OK. Level 2.
EVE	OK

EVE gently takes TABBY's arm and rubs her face gently on it, cat-like.

	Tabby?
TABBY	Mm?
EVE	What's humping? Is it like love?

51

TABBY   Really?
               We're going to do this now?

EVE   Plll/lllleeeeaaasse

TABBY   OK ok jesus just give me a
               OK
               OK

               Humping.

               So.
               So. You know Charlie?

EVE   Charlie the hamster?

TABBY   Charlie the hamster. Who we both loved
               very much.
               Until you ate him.

EVE   Yes?

TABBY   Well.
               When. When a mummy hamster and a
               daddy hamster love each other very much.
               But perhaps the mummy hamster has a
               headache or isn't really up for it and the
               daddy hamster finds it a bit difficult to
               restrain himself

	Or. You know if they happen to be two mummy hamsters
	Wait. No. This is a bit.
	Hang on.
	Dogs. You know dogs?
EVE	Like Cerberus?
TABBY	Er. I guess. They go 'woof'.
EVE	Yes.
TABBY	OK well dogs. Sometimes a little doggy loves his master's leg a bit too much. And And they might want to rub, or sort of Bounce on their master's leg a bit Because it feels nice
EVE	It does feel nice.
TABBY	Right. Right but you're not a dog you see Eve? You are not a dog. Understand?
EVE	OK.

TABBY	Ok so no more humping please. Ever. Oh God. I can't do this anymore.
EVE	Don't leave me.
TABBY	What? No I'm not. That's not I would never leave you Evee. Look at you. You're so Small.
EVE	I'm a monster
TABBY	You're not a monster you just You just need to be careful You know if you drink too much of my blood I'll turn into a vampire too. You know that don't you. In fact Maybe you should stop drinking my blood at all.
EVE	What?

TABBY   Maybe Eve, you should stop drinking my
               blood.

EVE   But I'll starve!

TABBY   Don't be silly vampires can't starve. Only
               three / things can

EVE   Only three things can kill vampires.
               Sunlight. Decapitation. A wooden stake
               hammered through the heart

TABBY   Right

EVE   But. But. The Hunger

TABBY   Well we could try other blood. Pig's blood?
               Or just you know raw meat?

EVE   Yuk

TABBY   Or jam sandwiches?
               You love jam sandwiches you eat them for
               dinner all the time

EVE   Only when you don't let me have Dinner
               dinner

TABBY   But there's other kinds of sandwiches Eve.
               So many kinds.

EVE   I like blood.

TABBY   Yeah well I've got none left to give Eve.

            I'm sorry but it's
            It's too dangerous.
            Do you want me to be a vampire?
            Do you?

EVE   No.

TABBY   No.

            And we can get rid of these fucking bins as
            well while we're at it.

EVE   But but rule number / 6 the

TABBY   I'm sick of cleaning up your shit Eve. I'm
            sick of it.

EVE   But if we break the rules

TABBY   We're not. We're not breaking the rules.
            We're changing the rules.

            Rule number six – you use the toilet. Like
            me.
            Like Tabby.

EVE   Toilet?
             But
             But that's outside the safe place.
             Rule number 1.

TABBY takes EVE's hand.

TABBY   Eve. Sweetie.

             There is more than one safe place.

             I promise.

EVE   Toilet is a safe place?

TABBY   Very safe. You'll see.

EVE   I can go into the castle?

TABBY   Yes. Into the CASTLE.

EVE   I can
             Explore.

TABBY   YES. Would you like to explore together?
             Because the whole castle is the safe place
             now.

EVE   Tabby. Can we just change all the rules?

And we won't have our spines injected with sulphuric acid or have our teeth pulled out?

TABBY   Eve. The thing about rules
          Rules are
          Who made the rules?

EVE   We did.

TABBY   OK so we can change them can't we?
          As long as we do it together.
          And we are very very careful.

EVE   I'm scared.

TABBY   I'm a little bit scared too.
          But
          It's exciting isn't it?

TABBY exits saying:

          We can do lots of new things.
          We could give you a proper bath

EVE   Yuk

TABBY re-enters holding a burka and a pair of tinted swimming goggles.

58

EVE	What's those?
TABBY	Eve You're good aren't you?
EVE	Yes.
TABBY	And we love each other very much.
EVE	Yes.
TABBY	Well if you're very very good. And you promise on your life not to talk to anyone Or you know Growl
EVE	Tabby?
TABBY	Eve Eve Would you like to go outside?

EVE stares at her.

[8]

The bins have gone. The room is cleaner.

EVE bursts onto stage, dressed in the burka and wearing the goggles. She is in the middle of a panic attack, tearing her clothes off.

EVE   It burns!

TABBY rushes on after her.

TABBY   Eve! EVE Jesus

EVE   I'm burning up!

EVE tears off the last of her clothes leaving her naked except for pants and swimming goggles.

TABBY   Eve you're going to give me a fucking panic attack in a minute

EVE   Downward Dog!

She adopts the position, breathing hard.

             I'm a bird I'm a bird I'm a robin I'm stork I'm a dove I'm a shape in the sky

TABBY   What the hell Eve?

EVE   You said it was safe!

TABBY   It is safe you're fine

EVE   The sun Tabby the eye of God burning me
                 alive the wind I couldn't breathe sucking
                 the air out of my lungs peeling all my skin

TABBY   EVE

EVE   The sky Tabby.
                 There was so much sky. It crushed me. It
                 swallowed me whole.

TABBY   OK.
                 OK Eve I'm going to get your clothes.
                 You look like a hermaphrodite swimming
                 champ.

TABBY exits.

EVE   I'm a phoenix. I'm a crow. I'm a guinea
                 fowl.

*TABBY returns with EVE's clothes, holding them out to her.
She checks her watch.*

TABBY   Come on Eve. You've got to get dressed.

EVE   You said there were no trees left.

TABBY   Now Eve you fucking *princess* I'm not
               standing here like a limp dick holding your
               fucking robes

EVE doesn't move.

EVE   No.

TABBY   What?

EVE   No.

TABBY   I haven't got time for this Eve

EVE   Why?

TABBY   OK.
               OK look.

               Close Your Eyes.

A beat. EVE relaxes. She closes her eyes.

               The magic's working.

               Where's the hole?

EVE places her hand over her solar plexus.

TABBY	Let me find you a soul.
	Here. Nice and fresh.
	It's warm. It's tiny and completely perfect.
	Shall I put it in.
	Eve?
EVE	Yes.
TABBY	In it goes.
	Can you feel it filling your body.
	Does it hurt?
EVE	A little.
TABBY	What?
EVE	It feels tight. Hot.
TABBY	OK.
	Here comes the mirror.
	Can you see?
EVE	I'm scared.
TABBY	Do you want to hold my hand?

She takes TABBY's hand.

	Shall we go outside?
EVE	I'm scared Tabby.
TABBY	Can you see the door? It's creaking open.
EVE	Sunlight!
TABBY	It doesn't burn you.
EVE	Close the door Tabby
TABBY	It's ok / Eve
EVE	CLOSE THE DOOR TABBY
TABBY	Jesus it's closed it's / closed
EVE	Take it out it hurts it hurts Tabby / it's hurting me
TABBY	It's out it's out
	There. There it goes. Gone.
	Jesus. Eve?

EVE   I don't want to go outside again Tabby.

TABBY   Eve

EVE   Like it here.
                Please Tabby.

TABBY   But
                But Eve if you never go outside, how are
                you going to find a Prince?

                Hm?

EVE   Rule number 3: Don't trust humans

TABBY   Except for Tabby

EVE   And definitely not BOYS.

TABBY   Well.
                Some boys are different.

EVE stares at her.

EVE   You said

TABBY   I know what I said

EVE   They

TABBY	I know
EVE	With their
TABBY	Eve listen. Someone is coming here.
EVE	Rule number
TABBY	We changed the rules remember?
EVE	Not that one not all the rules
TABBY	Eve please. Listen. This I'm going to tell you something and I want you to think about it. Have a good think because it's a good thing. I promise you it's a good thing. I've I've met someone.
EVE	A boy?!
TABBY	Yes.
EVE	What did you do to him?

TABBY   What? No. No I
               I think I love him Eve.

EVE is aghast.

               He's
               He's coming here. Tonight.

EVE   No!

TABBY   Yes because I'm a fucking idiot!
               I was hoping

EVE   Rule number

TABBY   He's not coming upstairs. Jesus no. We'll
               just

EVE   Rule number

TABBY   EVE PLEASE
               Please don't fuck this up for me.

               I'm
               I don't really know I've no idea what I'm
               doing. I need you
               I need you not to make it any worse.

She looks at her watch

Oh fuck and I'm supposed to be cooking
dinner fuck fuck
What do boys eat?

EVE   Tabby

TABBY   Eve shush for a minute. Let me think.

EVE   Can I

TABBY   Eve

EVE   Can I see him?

*TABBY looks at EVE. She is still naked, wearing the goggles,
clutching her clothes like a doll.*

TABBY   Um. Not tonight.
                But soon! Soon yes. That's
                I would like that.

EVE   Can I smell him?
                Just a bit?

TABBY   Eve. Another time. Of course you can.
                Maybe. I'm sure he'd

                We'll talk about it later ok you've got to
                get dressed.

EVE   Too hot

TABBY   EVE

EVE   Brrr chilly.

She begins to get dressed. TABBY exits and returns with a dog leash.

                Not The Leash.

TABBY   I'm sorry Evee. It's just for tonight. I
                promise.

She puts it on EVE and ties her to the bed.

                You've not been bad. Understand? You've
                not done anything wrong.
                I just can't have you fucking this up.
                Understand?

EVE   Not really.

She looks at EVE.

TABBY   What the fuck am I going to cook?

EVE watches her.

                What the fuck am I doing?

69

EVE   Don't be scared Tabby.
                You're very pretty.

TABBY   Thank you.

                I do love you Eve.

EVE   I love you.

                Tabby?

TABBY   What?

EVE   Cuddles?

TABBY   Eve
                OK. Level 1.

EVE wraps her arms round herself and squeezes.

EVE   Mmmm.

TABBY stares at her.

TABBY   Veal.
                Fuck it. I'll do veal.

[9]

EVE has her ear pressed to the floor. TABBY is seated at dinner with Steve.

TABBY   Ta dah!
      Veal!

EVE   I can hear him. Feel his rumble.
      Throbbing voices.

      Makes me tremble.

      I wonder what he looks like
      Dark or Fair
      Prince Charming or Prince Handsome

TABBY   Oh shit.
      I bet you're vegetarian aren't you? You've
      got that floppy sort of thing that
      vegetarians
      Are you sure?
      Because I'll have yours and you can have
      Fucking lentils and pond water or
      whatever it is you people eat.

      Sorry. I don't entertain very much.
      Or at all.

71

EVE   Don't   think   Tabby   would   choose
             Charming over Handsome.

TABBY   I
             Hey
             I want to have an abortion.

             But I can't seem to get pregnant.

             It's a joke. A

             I knew you wouldn't find it funny.
             You don't feel entitled to laugh because
             you've never had one.

             Oh my god I'm terrible at this I don't
             I don't do this.

EVE   Rapunzel just let down her hair and the
             Prince climbed up.
             My hair is...

TABBY   Oh it's hardly a castle Steve. Although I
             admit the table looks like it belongs in
             fucking Camelot. It's just a big, quite a big
             house.
             And I didn't buy it by the way, Daddy left
             it in his will. Along with all his money and
             six tonnes of neuroses.

So he must have loved me deep down. Ha
ha.
Oh mummy ran off with a cunt in a
Porsche when I was ten and Daddy
devolved into this spiteful, bitter

He kept me on a short leash after that.
Terrified I'd turn into a slut like Mummy.

So of course I did.
Ha ha.

EVE   Don't need to be a princess to get a prince.

TABBY   I did warn you Steve.

EVE begins to scratch on the floor. TABBY can hear it.

EVE   I'll call him.
             And he'll come to me.

TABBY   It's just mice. Ignore it.

             I mean
             We all do stupid things when we're fifteen
             right? You must have
             The stupid thing I did just happened to
             work with Daddy.
             Not that he believed me when I told him
             who the father was. I mean who would

believe the spawn of a scheming whore like
Mummy?

More veal?

EVE   When he sees me he'll scream and try to
get away.
He won't understand.
But I'll break his legs. Give him all my
love. Suck him dry.
Make him mine.

The scratching gets louder.

TABBY   Fucking mice! They'll be the death of me I
swear.
Anyway look. Can we
God why are you even still here? Shouldn't
you be running for the hills or
This was a bad idea.

No it was.

Let's talk about you for bit. I'm dying
here.
Thank you. I'm not really much of cook
We just live on sandwiches here.
We
The royal we, you know?
I live in a castle after all!

EVE   I'll sing to him. Like a Siren.
               He'll stay forever.
               And I'll hump him as much as I like.

She begins to sing alluringly – or what she imagines is alluringly.

TABBY listens, frozen.

TABBY   Yes I know mice don't sing Steven. I left
               the fucking radio on alright?
               I'll just go and deal with it.
               Finish your veal, it nearly killed me.

TABBY storms in.

EVE   What's the password.

TABBY   What the fuck do you think you're playing
               at?

EVE   You didn't use the password

TABBY   I don't need a fucking password this is my
               house
               Why are you being a little bitch?

EVE   Hungry.

TABBY storms out and returns with sandwiches.

75

TABBY   There.

EVE   No.
               HUNGRY.

TABBY   Don't fuck with me Eve.

EVE deliberately raises her voice.

EVE   HUNGRY!

TABBY   Fine.

TABBY exits, returns with duct tape and oven gloves. She tapes the oven gloves to EVE's hands.

TABBY   You're not the only monster in this house
               Eve.
               Remember that.

She sticks a piece of duct tape over EVE's mouth and exits.

[10]

EVE sits very still, the tape still on her mouth, the leash still round her neck, staring at the door. She could be made of stone.

A door closes, somewhere in the house.

TABBY   9-7-5-3

               9-7-5-3

               Eve?

She enters. Sees EVE.

               Oh yeah.

She dumps the bags of shopping she is carrying.
She goes to EVE and takes off the duct tape.

               I'm sorry Evee.

               Cuddles?

She takes the over-gloves off EVE's hands.
She undoes the leash.

               Better?

               Are you having a think?

EVE   You left.

TABBY   Yes.

EVE   One hundred and nineteen thousand five
             hundred and twenty-two heartbeats.

TABBY   I'm so sorry Evee.
             Cuddles? Make it better?

EVE   Level 1.

TABBY   Only Level 1?

EVE   OK. Level 2.

She holds out an arm. TABBY takes it, strokes it.

EVE   I don't want new rules.
             I liked the old rules.

TABBY   I know but

EVE   I'm not a princess like you.

TABBY   I don't know Evee.
             I don't know.

             I bought you something.

EVE   What?

TABBY   Do you want to see it?

TABBY goes to a bag and pulls out a nice dress.

EVE   What is it?

TABBY   What is it? It's a fucking dress Eve.
             A pretty dress.
             For you.

EVE   Why?

TABBY   To say sorry.
             It's a sorry dress.

             You could put it on now if you like?
             I could get a mirror

EVE   Don't show up in mirrors duh.

TABBY   Of course. Sorry.
             Well.
             Do you want to put it on anyway?

TABBY helps her put it on.
Looks at her, visibly moved.

             You look

EVE   What?
                What's wrong?

TABBY   You look. You look lovely.
                Really lovely.

EVE   Don't cry Tabby I'll take it off

TABBY   No don't
                Don't.
                Eve you're very precious to me you've
                been everything to me since the day you
                were born I'm sorry
                I'm sorry things are the way they are

EVE   I like it.

TABBY   But Eve
                You could be
                We
                I've made a lot of mistakes. I could do
                things so much better. Things could be so
                much better.

                You know if you just had a bath

EVE   No.

TABBY   You'd like having baths Eve you could
                look so pretty

EVE   What mistakes?

TABBY   Just
               It doesn't matter now.

EVE   I'm hungry.

TABBY   I made you jam sandwiches.

EVE   Don't like jam.

TABBY   Oh Eve you fucking LOVE jam! You've
               being getting through a pot of jam a week
               since you were twelve!

EVE   Don't like jam.

TABBY   OK

*TABBY goes over to her bags and starts to pull out
sandwiches.*

TABBY   OK
               Cheese. Cheese and onion. BLT. Bumper
               bloody Breakfast. Chorizo and fucking
               lemongrass. Peanut butter. Jam. Peanut
               butter AND jam.
               A whole new world.

EVE   I want Dinner dinner.

TABBY   We've talked about this is. You need to
          learn.
          I can't give you any more blood. It is
          killing me.
          And you don't need blood. Not really. Not
          need.
          You're just
          You're an addict.
          And it's time to go cold turkey.

She delves into the bag and pulls out another sandwich.

          Cold turkey and cranberry in fact.

          Eat it.

          Eat it.

          I can wait all day Eve.

          Look.

She takes a bite out of the sandwich.
She chews with disguised revulsion. She checks the package
suspiciously.

          Jesus fucking Christ…

Swallows.

Yummy.
Your turn.

Oh for fuck's sake.
Look.

She holds the sandwich high in the air and begins to swoop it slowly towards EVE.

Here comes the aeroplane into the airport.

EVE   What's an aeroplane?

TABBY   Here comes the
                Dragon.

                Here comes the dragon swooping towards
                the
                The Magic Cave.

The sandwich comes to a stop in front of EVE's firmly clamped mouth.

You have to open the Magic Cave Eve.
You need to open the cave Eve or the
dragon will smash into the mountain.

Fine.

She starts the descent again.

Here comes the dragon swooping towards the magic cave.
Oh dear looks like he might crash.
Is the magical cave going to open?

She pushes the sandwich firmly into EVE's face, smearing it all over her.

Oh shit. He's crashed. He's smashed himself all over the magical mountain.
And the mountain looks fucking stupid now.

EVE   I miss Mummy.

TABBY   No you don't.

EVE   Need the red bin.

TABBY   You need the toilet?

EVE   Red bin.

TABBY   No. Toilet.

TABBY takes off the collar.

Come on. Let's go to the toilet. We can clean you up too.

EVE	No.
	Red bin.
TABBY	It's just outside come on.
EVE	No.
TABBY	EVE
EVE	Get red bin.
TABBY	I'll give you fucking red bin.

TABBY exits.
A beat.
She bursts back in wielding a crucifix.
EVE screams.

	I warned you Eve I fucking warned you.
EVE	Tabby stop!
TABBY	Eat your sandwiches / Eve
EVE	Please Tabby! Please Rule / Number 11
TABBY	The power of Christ compels you to eat your fucking / sandwiches
EVE	Tabby! Tabby! Please!

85

TABBY pauses.

TABBY   Oh for fuck's sake.

EVE is crying.

                  Not in the dress. Not in the nice new dress.

EVE has soiled herself.

EVE   Told you.

TABBY   I just
                  I just
                  One thing. Just one nice thing.

                  It doesn't matter. It doesn't matter what I
                  do, everything. Everything always ends up
                  covered in shit.

EVE   I don't want nice things I just want you

TABBY   I want you to be happy Eve.
                  But I can't
                  I can't can I

EVE   I was happy.

TABBY   I wish

EVE   You wished for me

TABBY   I wish

EVE   Tabby don't

TABBY   I wish you hadn't been born Eve.

EVE   Tabby?

           Don't leave please.

TABBY   I can't

EVE   Tabby?

TABBY   I'm sorry Eve I

She runs out.

EVE   Tabby?

[11]

TABBY is in a café.

TABBY   It was inevitable really.

EVE   It couldn't last.

TABBY   I had a bear. Mummy gave it to me when I
was still little and she still gave a shit.
It was her bear. And she had got it from
her Mum.
This bear had seen two world wars and it
looked like shit.

EVE   Can't trust humans.
Rule number 3.
Can't trust food.

TABBY   This bear had been cuddled to death. This
bear was practically family.
Then Mummy and I had a fight. When I
was about five. About something stupid
and
Out of spite
I was a spiteful child, you can imagine
I grabbed it by the head. That head that
smelled of three generations of soundly
sleeping girls. With those glass eyes that
had stared blank love at me all my life.

88

I grabbed that soft, care-worn head and I
pulled it off.
And threw it on the fire.

And then I cried and cried and cried
Daddy scoured the shops and got a new
head that fitted it might even have been
the exact same model but
Of course it wasn't the same. The fur was
new, the smell was gone. There was no love
in those blank eyes.

I break things Steve. It is the closest thing
I have to a personality trait.
And some things can't be fixed.

EVE   Stupid. Pretending to be a princess.
The ugly duckling was never going to be a
duck. Was never meant to be.
A thing can't be another thing or nothing
would ever be anything.
There wouldn't be any monsters. They'd
all choose to be something else.

TABBY   You're unbelievable. You're ridiculous.
         Precious. You don't belong in this world.
         It's like watching a fucking unicorn prance
         about London.
         With your little twat bib on.
         And I refuse.
         I absolutely refuse to break you too.

EVE   She had to leave.
         Humans and monsters can't live together.
         Not forever. Not alive.

TABBY   No.
         I've already made my decision.
         No I don't want to talk about it I can't.

         Don't be stupid. Don't give me that shit.
         Honesty. God. Of all the retarded...
         That's one of the things you read about in
         your fucking Cosmo magazine isn't it?
         It's air. It has no reality.
         You really think honesty is what makes
         things work?

         You think it was hard telling you about
         my abortion?
         I mean Jesus, who hasn't had a fucking
         abortion these days? You know something
         like a third of women will suffer rape at

some point in their lives? You think I'm worried about that shit?
You don't know anything about me Steve.

EVE   I was right to hide my gifts.
             Now
             Now I don't need her

EVE goes to look under the bed.

TABBY   You want to try a bit of honesty Steve?
             OK how about the fact that Daddy tried to do my abortion himself? Didn't think it was anybody else's business. On that kitchen table actually.
             He didn't do a great job.

             And that's just the stuff I'm prepared to tell you.
             In a fucking Costa Coffee.

             Trust me Steve. I've got skeletons in my closet that could rip you arm off.
             So don't talk to me about honesty.

EVE   They're still here. I collected every one.
             Kept them safe.
             For emergencies.

TABBY   You

You almost got me. You almost had me believing. You sneak.
You were a crack in the wall. You let light in. Just a sliver.
A little bit of air.

No don't.

TABBY   I
            I know. And look
            I'm not saying I don't love you
            I do love you Steve.

EVE   I thought I loved her but that's impossible.
            Vampires don't love.

TABBY   I love people
            Like hammers love nails.

EVE   Vampires feed.

TABBY   No stop.
            Stop.
            Stop.
            Don't follow me. Delete my number.
            Stay away from me Steve I mean it.
            I warned you. I fucking warned you

            Here be monsters

[12]

TABBY   9-7-5-3

               Eve?

TABBY enters.
EVE is nowhere to be seen.

               Eve?

EVE   I'm hiding.

TABBY   Come out Eve. I need to talk to you.

EVE   You came back.

TABBY   Of course I came back.
               I always do.
               I always will.

               He's gone Eve. He won't come here
               anymore.
               I promise.

EVE   Really?

TABBY   Really.
               I'm sorry for what I said.

EVE   What about the rules?

TABBY   Let's keep the rules.
             Shall we?

EVE   Yeah.

TABBY   I thought
             I just thought I could make things better
             but I made them worse instead.
             I was stupid.

EVE   You're not stupid Tabby.

TABBY   Are we friends again?

EVE   OK

TABBY   I'm sorry I scared you with a crucifix.

EVE   I'm sorry I pooed in your dress.

TABBY   I can clean it.
             You could
             You can still wear it if you want to.

             Eve?

EVE   I like things the way they were.

TABBY   Things can be the same they were. But
               better. Maybe.

               Eve?

               I could do with a cuddle.

EVE emerges from under the bed, her lips smeared with blood.

               Fuck!

EVE makes to hug TABBY who flinches away.

               Eve? Tell me that's jam. Please tell me it's
               jam.

EVE   It's jam.

TABBY   It's not fucking jam Eve you liar what
               have you done?

               What have you done Eve?

EVE   Was hungry.

TABBY   So?

EVE   So

TABBY   So?

EVE	So
TABBY	EVE
EVE	I thought you weren't coming back.
TABBY	What did you do Eve?
EVE	I ate some.
TABBY	Ate what Eve? Ate. What?
EVE	Don't need you anymore. I've got my gifts.
TABBY	Gifts?
EVE	From me. I collected them. Every one. Stopped them escaping.
TABBY	Oh god. Eve. Eve Listen to me Where are your gifts?
EVE	Under the bed.

TABBY darts away.

| TABBY | Jesus!
Eve what is under that bed tell me now |
|---|---|
| EVE | My gifts |
| TABBY | Are they
Do they bite? |
| EVE | No silly. |
| TABBY | OK.
OK Eve.
I want you to show me. |
| EVE | All of them? |
| TABBY | No! God. Just one. Very slowly. |

EVE reaches under the bed and slowly pulls out a jam jar.
She shows it to TABBY. Inside is a used tampon.

| TABBY | Oh
Oh fucking Christ |
|---|---|
| EVE | Tabby? |
| TABBY | No don't touch me |

TABBY exits.
EVE puts the jar gently back under the bed.

TABBY re-enters with her hands behind her back. Her eyes are closed.

TABBY   I am
                     I'm a leaf I'm a leaf
                     I'm a fucking leaf on fucking tranquil ocean.

EVE   Tabby

TABBY   Shut up Eve. I'm talking now.

                     Eve.
                     Sweetie.
                     Listen very carefully.

                     You
                     Are not a vampire.

                     I repeat. You are not a vampire.
                     You are a human being.
                     You do not need to drink blood.
                     You can drink Fanta. You can eat garlic if you want.
                     Listen Eve.
                     You are a normal teenage girl.
                     You don't crave blood you crave you crave bigger breasts and an iPad.
                     Are you listening?

EVE   What's an iPad

TABBY   LISTEN
             Vampires don't exist Evee. Phoenixes and
             giants and demons don't exist.
             Money exists. Chavs exist. Buses and
             Tesco and fucking politicians exist.

EVE   You're lying.

TABBY   No.

*She gives her the mirror from behind her back. EVE is
transfixed.*

             You're not a vampire Evee.
             I mean.
             Look at you.

EVE   No.

TABBY   Can you see?
             That's you Evee. That's you.

             Sunlight won't hurt you. People won't
             hurt you.
             We can go outside together, right now

EVE   Don't touch me!

TABBY   I had to Evee. You've got to understand I
           was a child I was
           Daddy said I should

EVE   Daddy?

TABBY   My Daddy Eve. My Daddy.
           You weren't meant to happen you weren't
           meant to survive
           I just wanted to protect you.

EVE   I remember Daddy remember his shadow

TABBY   Not your Daddy. You never met your
           Daddy.
           I told you about him

EVE   No

TABBY   Yes Evee. You wanted to know about the
           Mr Wallace.

EVE   Rule number 7

TABBY   I'm so sorry Evee.

EVE   You're a liar I remember I remember
           Mummy

TABBY   Do you?

EVE	She She fed me
TABBY	I fed you Eve. I've always fed you. No one knows you exist. But you do. You do exist Evee. Evee?
EVE	Vampires can't cry.
TABBY	OK.
EVE	Cuddles?
TABBY	Of course sweetie of course.
EVE	Level 5.

They embrace. EVE sinks her teeth into TABBY's neck.

[13]

EVE is lashed to the bed again.

TABBY enters. She has a bandage around her neck. She is holding a Frisbee.
They look at each other.

EVE   Don't need a password anymore.

TABBY   No.
              We don't.

EVE   No more rules.

              You look funny.

TABBY   Got pretty funny looks from the doctor.
              Told him it was a shaving accident. Har
              har.

              You could have killed me Eve.

EVE   You taste good.

TABBY   Stop it.

EVE   Can you feel it? Taking over
              It starts with a fever.
              Then the Hunger.

TABBY   Stop it Eve.
               That's not going to happen. I promise you.

               I've had a think.

EVE   Good think or bad think?

TABBY   Good think.

She raises the Frisbee. EVE is a bit scared.

EVE   What's that?

TABBY   This
               Is a Frisbee.

EVE   What does it do?

TABBY   It's a game Eve.

               You're going to come outside and we are
               going to throw it around.
               It will be Fun.
               And then you will see that I'm not lying
               any more.
               And then we can be a family. A normal
               family.

EVE   Can't go outside.

TABBY   Things can be different Eve.
         I learned that. So can you. Things can
         change.

EVE   Why does it have to change?

TABBY   This is better Eve. You could do anything.
         You can be whoever you want to be now.
         You can be happy.
         You just have to come with me.

         You have to trust me Eve.

EVE   I liked it the way it was.

TABBY   It wasn't right Eve.

EVE   I liked it. I liked you.

TABBY   I still like you. I love you.

EVE   You Fear Me.

TABBY   Oh fucking come on Eve it'll be fun look

*She throws the Frisbee. It lands by EVE – it might even hit
her.*
They both look at it on the floor.

EVE   Not that fun.

TABBY	You have to throw it back.
EVE	No. Come and get it.
TABBY	
EVE	See?
TABBY	Eve. I finally have a chance to be happy. We both do.
EVE	I am happy.
TABBY	You're confused Eve.
EVE	I was. You tried to make me human but you can't. I know what I am now.
TABBY	Eve I know. Close Your Eyes.
EVE	No.
TABBY	Eve it's easy just close your eyes and pretend.

EVE   No.

TABBY   That's all I do Eve. That's all anyone does.
               Do you think it's easy being human all the
               time?

EVE   I don't WANT to be human

TABBY   Fuck's sake Eve you don't have a choice
               you are human!

EVE   How can you tell?

TABBY   Because vampires don't fucking exist Eve

EVE   Prove it.

TABBY   If you just come outside

EVE   And burn to death.

TABBY   No!

EVE   I know why you're trying to kill me, I
               understand.

TABBY   I'm trying to save you Eve! I want us to
               be a family.
               You me
               And Steve.

EVE   OK

TABBY   OK?

EVE   Make a deal.

TABBY   A deal?
           OK a deal. What deal?

EVE   I'll come outside with you
           After
           After you bring Steve to me.

           Let me see him. Smell him.
           Let me feed on him.
           Suck him dry.

           And if he doesn't turn. I'll know you were
           telling the truth.
           This time.

           And we can go play with the frrz-bee.

TABBY   Fuck you Eve. He's mine.

           Here's a deal
           Here's a fucking deal Eve.
           Come with me now, outside.

Come and play Frisbee now or I swear to
God I will brick up this room and leave
you here to rot.

EVE laughs.

I'm not joking Eve, don't think I'm
fucking joking because I promise I promise
you

Have a good think.

EVE   Only three ways to kill a vampire

TABBY   Eve

EVE   Sunlight. Decapitation

TABBY   Eve

EVE   Hammer a wooden stake through the
                heart.

TABBY   Eve you're not a vampire. You will die.
                And no one will ever know you even
                existed.

                Now make a choice.

                Eve?

108

EVE	You'll know.
TABBY	Eve.
EVE	You'll know.
TABBY	Eve. Choose.
EVE	Cuddles?
TABBY	

EVE raises her arms towards TABBY entreatingly.

[14]

TABBY is alone. EVE is gone. The room is gone.

And the monster was locked away forever
Where it could do no harm. As was right.

Very faintly, a scratching sound begins to build.

The cherished Princess married her Prince the very next
day.
And they lived together in the castle until they were both
old and grey.

And all through years
Every now and then
They heard a strange
Scratching sound.

It's just mice they said.

It's just mice.

The scratching sound is much louder.

And they lived happily ever after.

More or less.

The scratching has become almost deafening.

End.